MOTOR SKILLS

A-Z

By Erick and Lisa Blore

TRUCK COLORING BOOK

Strong fine motor skills set kids up to experience greater success with less frustration as they learn to write. Moreover, coloring pictures they love is a fun way to entice reluctant writers to practice these skills.

Please note, the "Driving Skills" sections are not intended to teach precise letter formation, but to be a fun way to practice the basic shapes involved in writing.

Copyright © 2019 Erick and Lisa Blore

ISBN 978-0-9834906-2-3

Published by Eclectry Books

Ambulance

Driving Skills

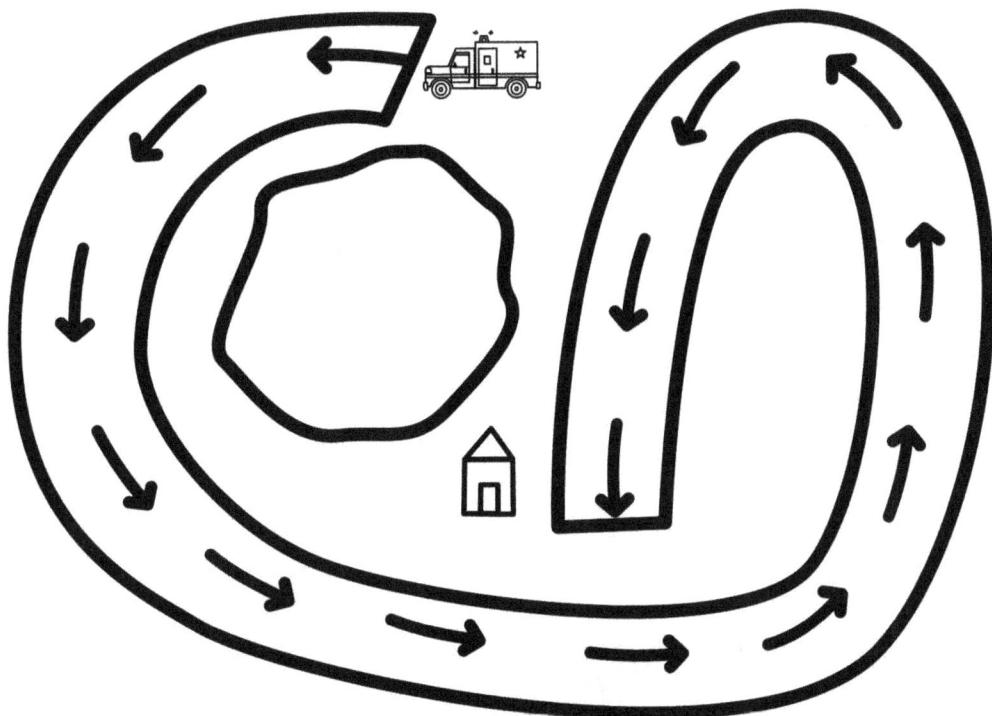

Ambulance

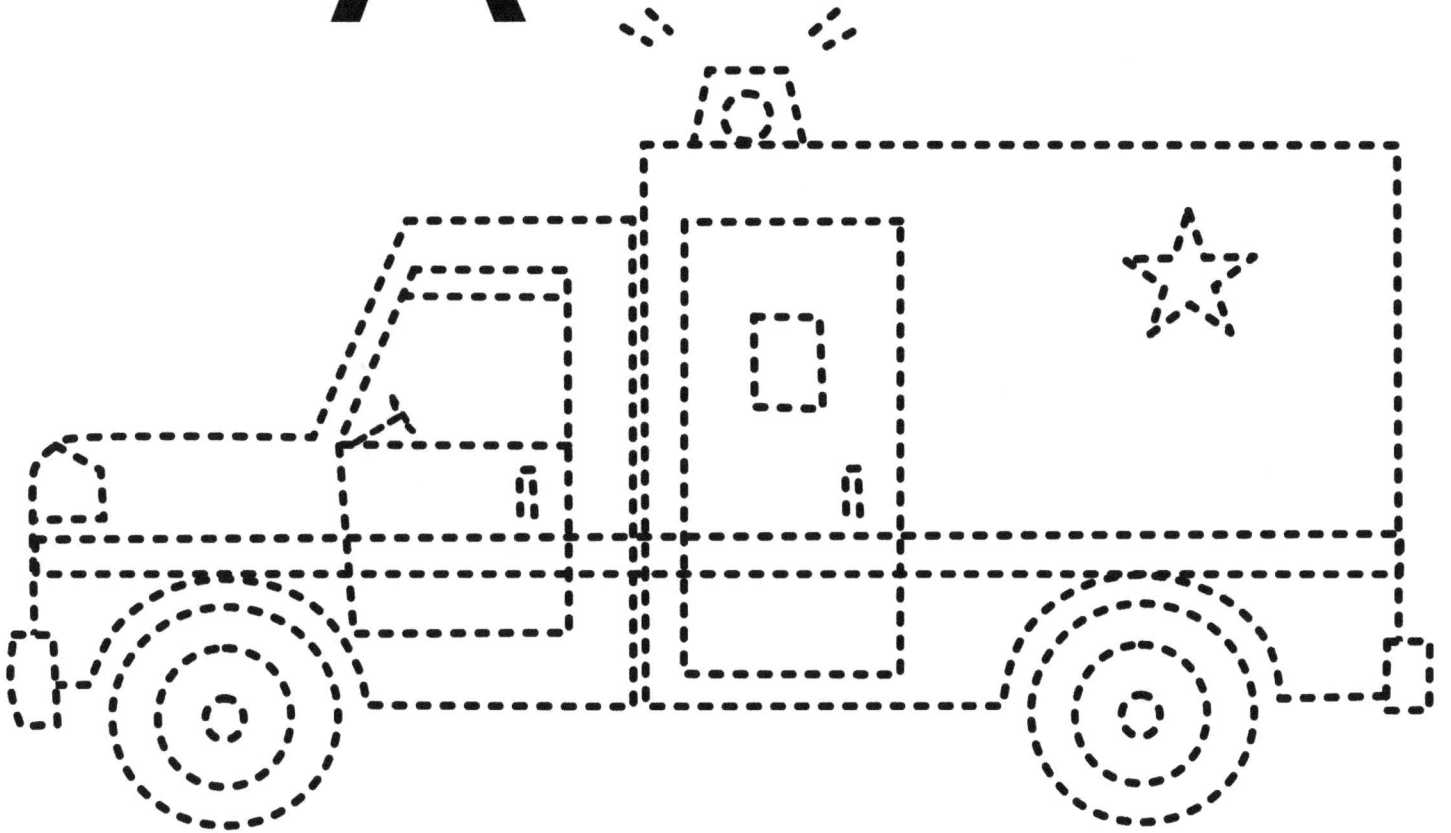

Trace.

Draw your own ambulance.

Bulldozer

Driving Skills

Bulldozer

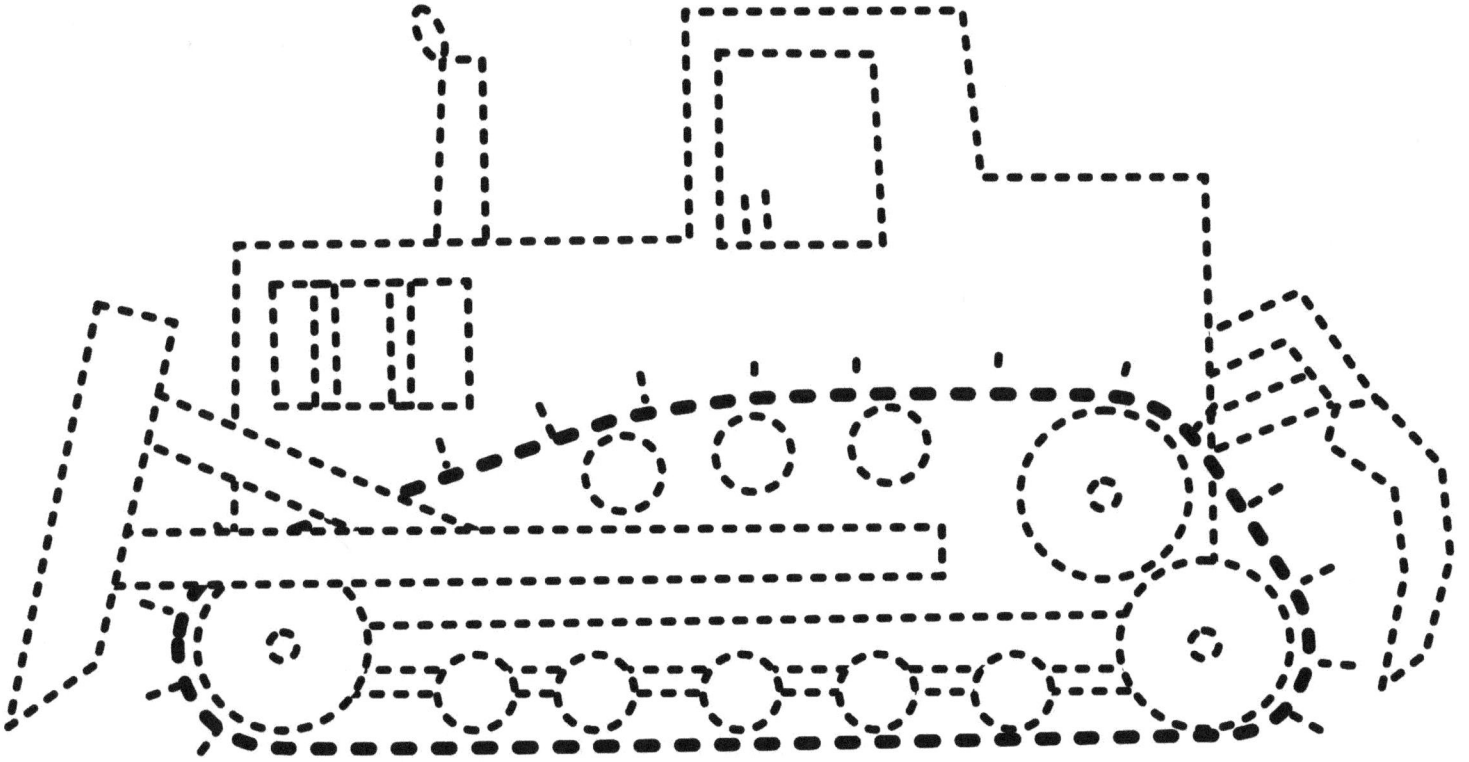

Trace.

Draw your own bulldozer.

Concrete Mixer

Driving Skills

Concrete Mixer

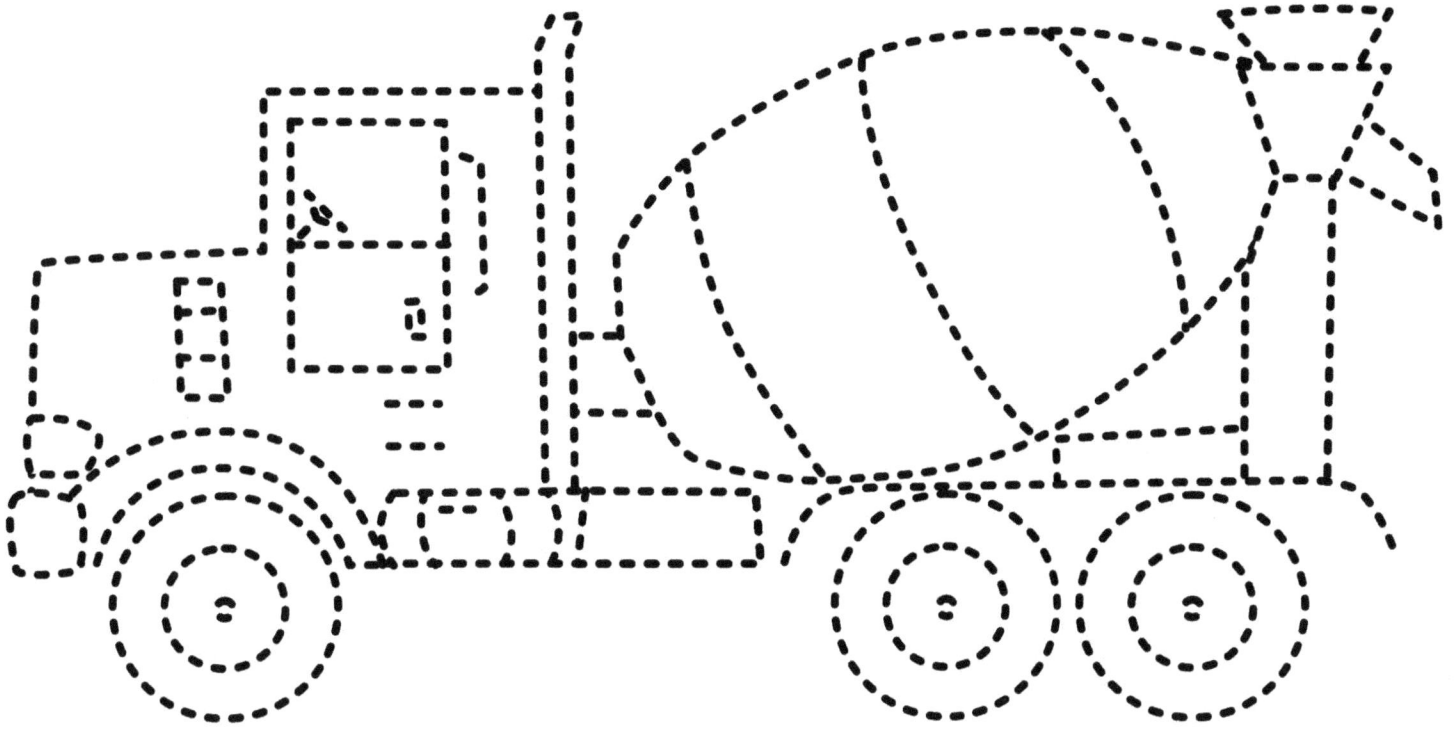

Trace.

Draw your own concrete mixer.

Dump Truck

Driving Skills

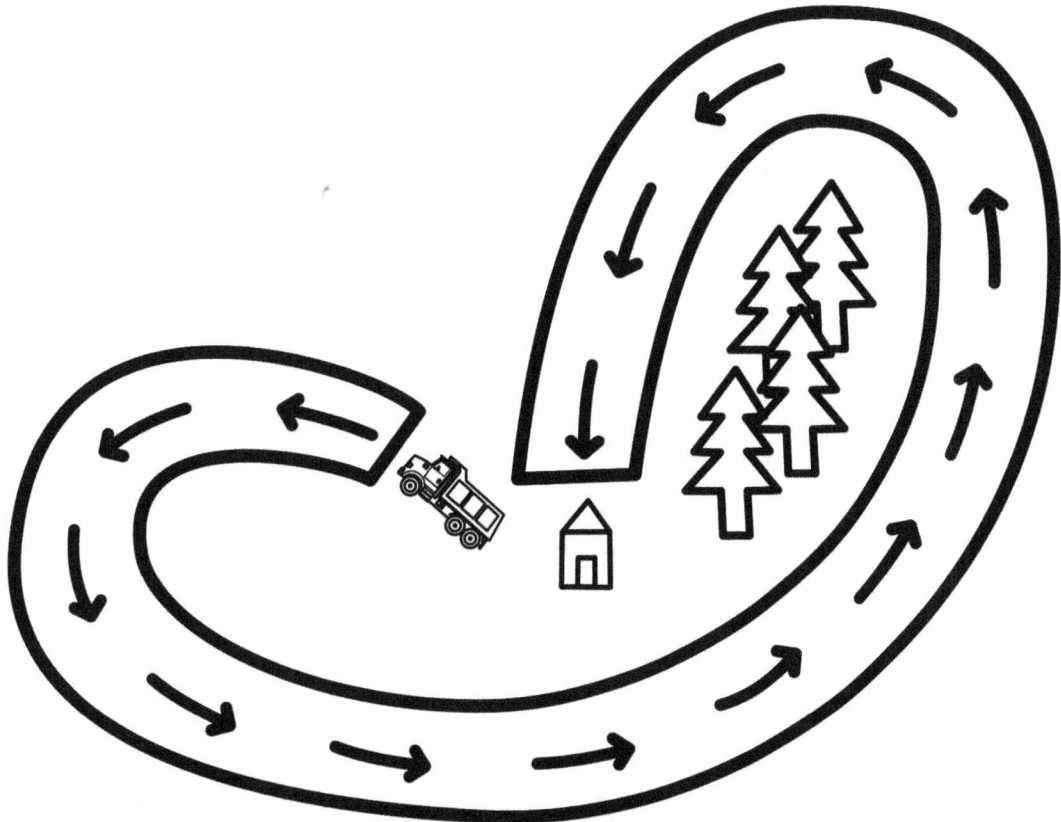

Dump Truck

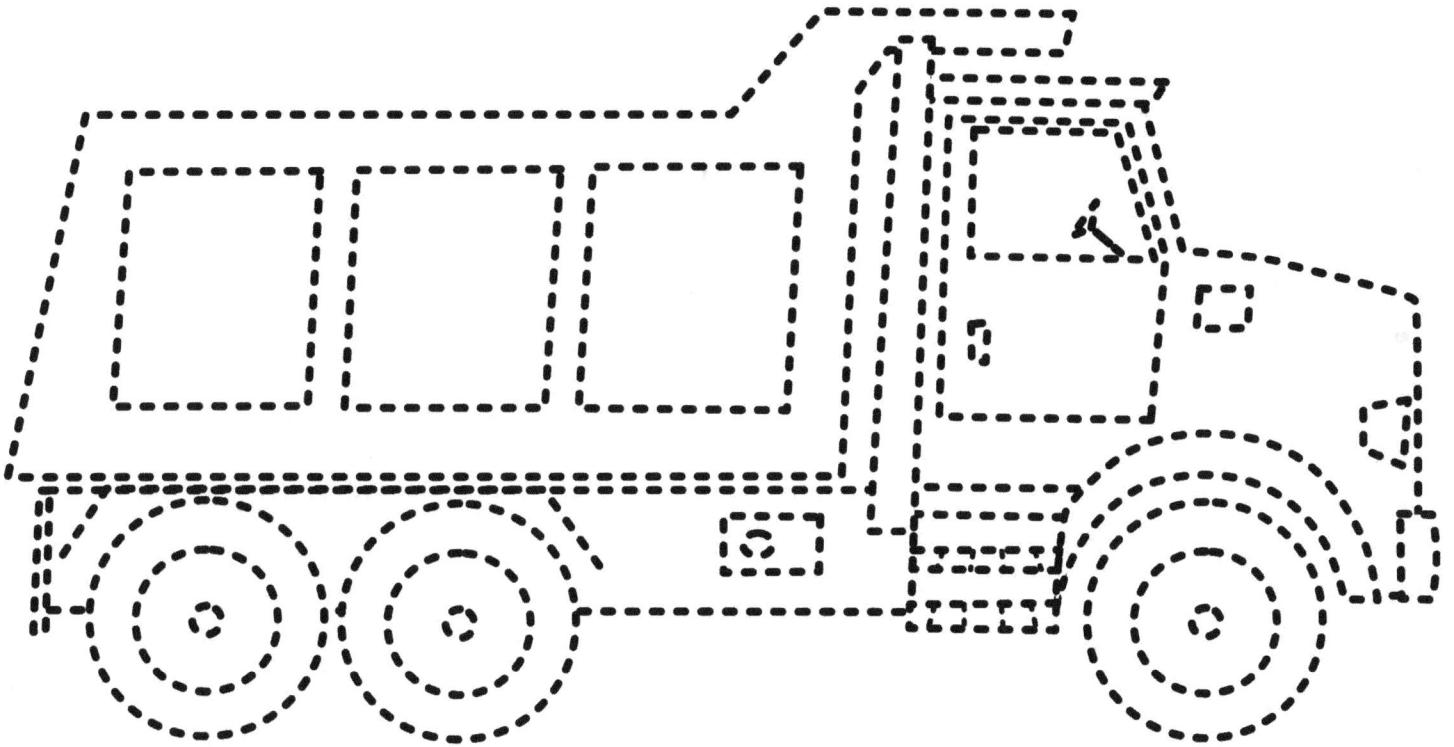

Trace.

Draw your own dump truck.

Excavator

Driving Skills

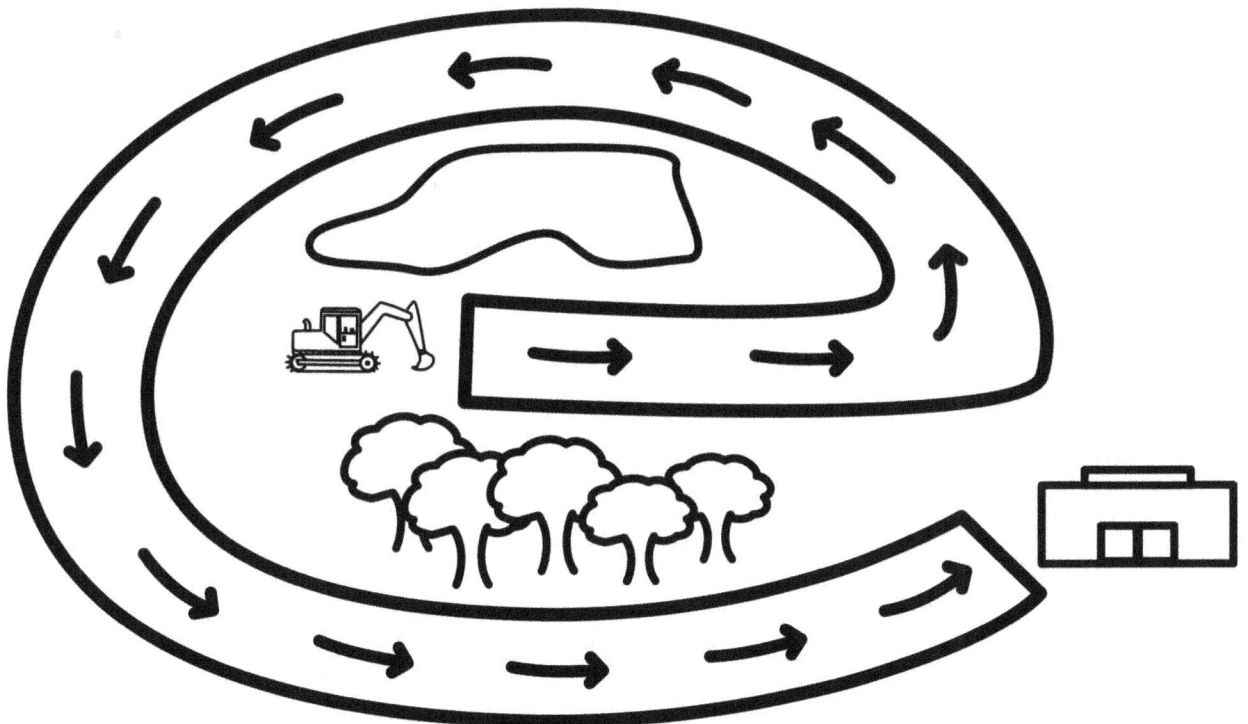

Excavator

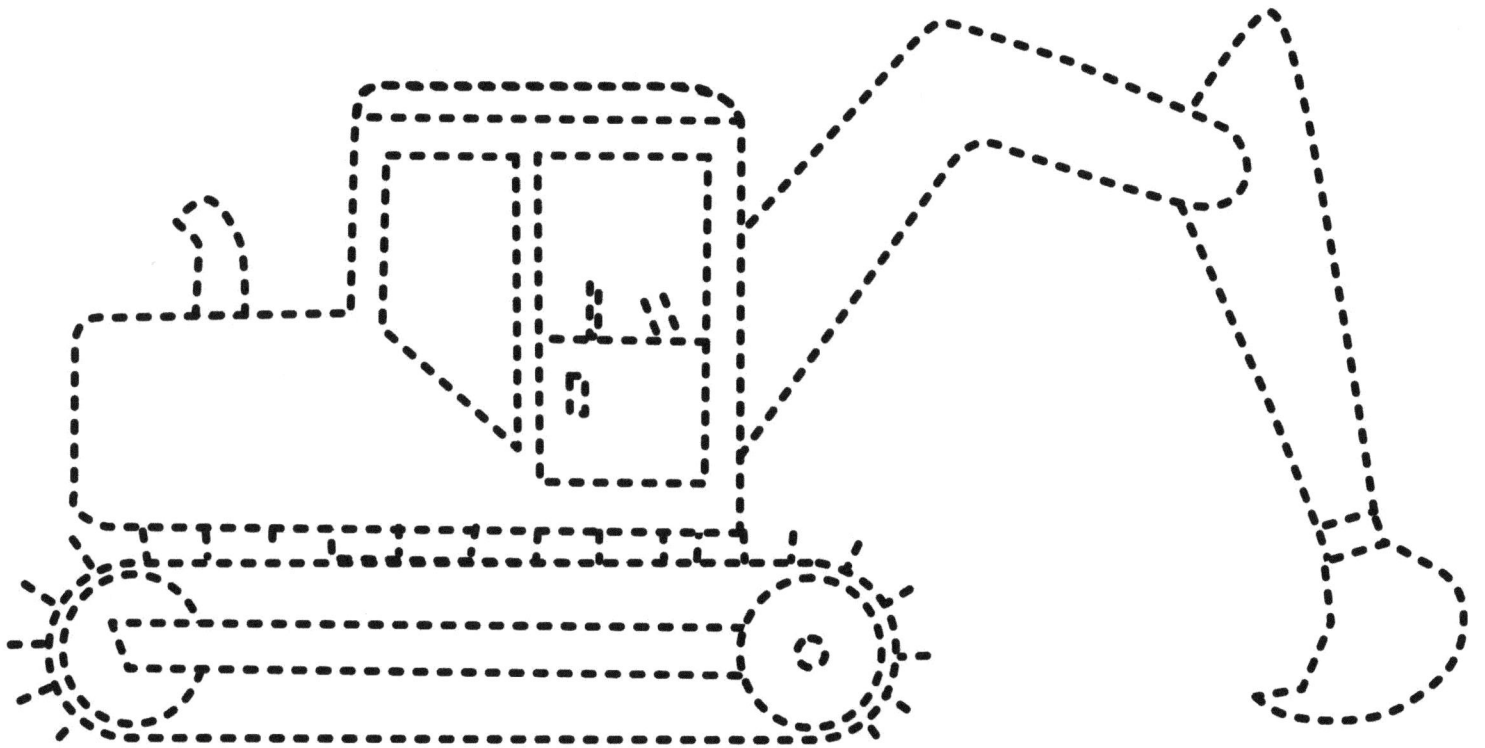

Trace.

Draw your own excavator.

Fire Truck

Driving Skills

Fire Truck

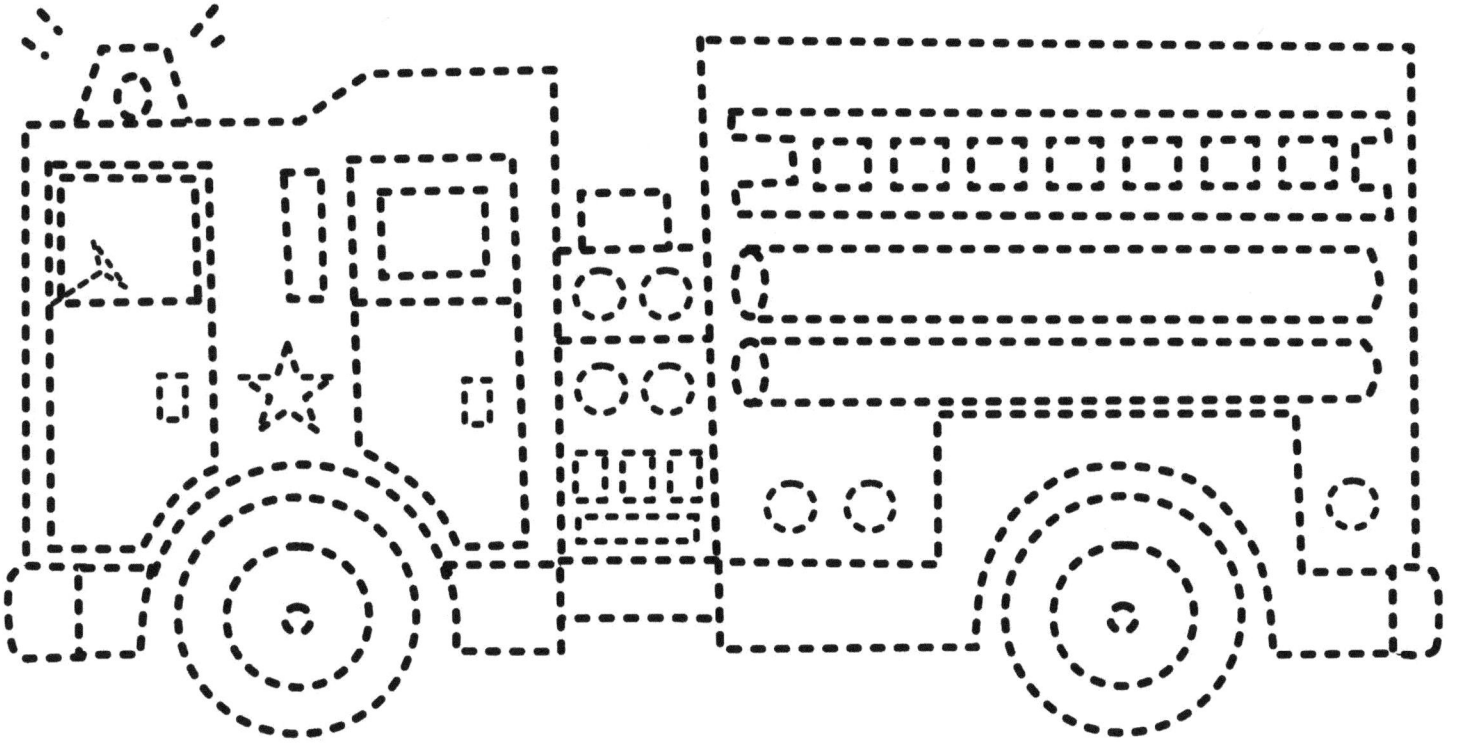

Trace.

Draw your own fire truck.

Garbage Truck

Driving Skills

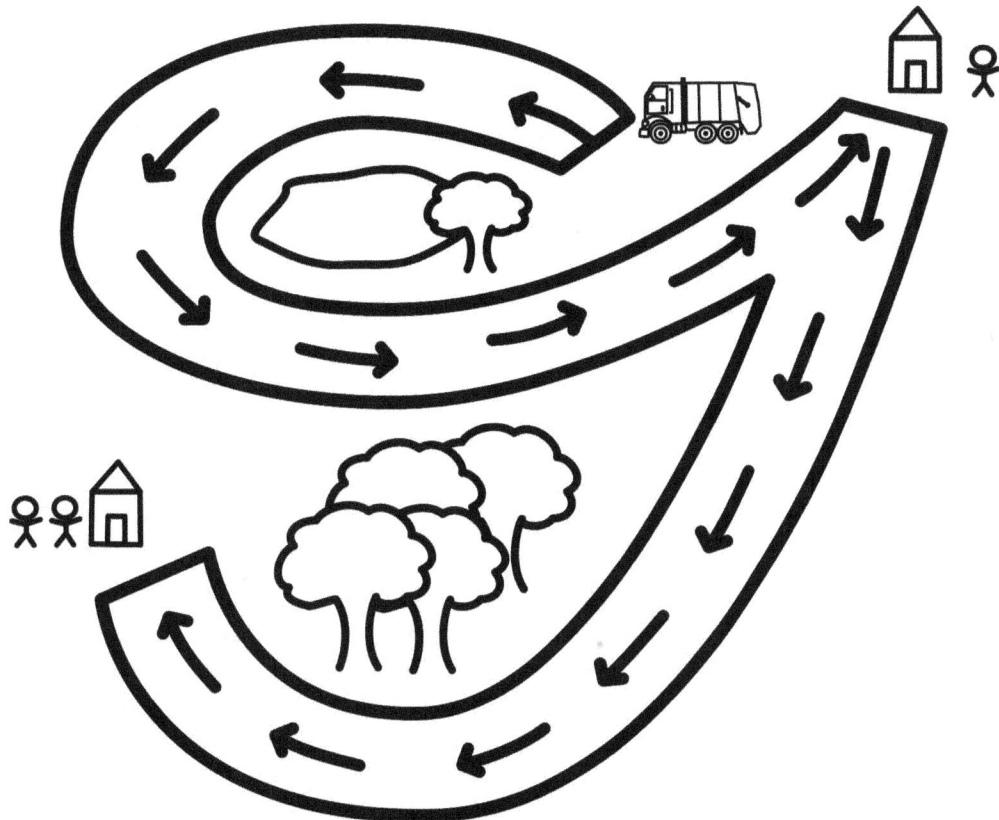

Garbage Truck

Trace.

Draw your own garbage truck.

Harvester

Driving Skills

Harvester

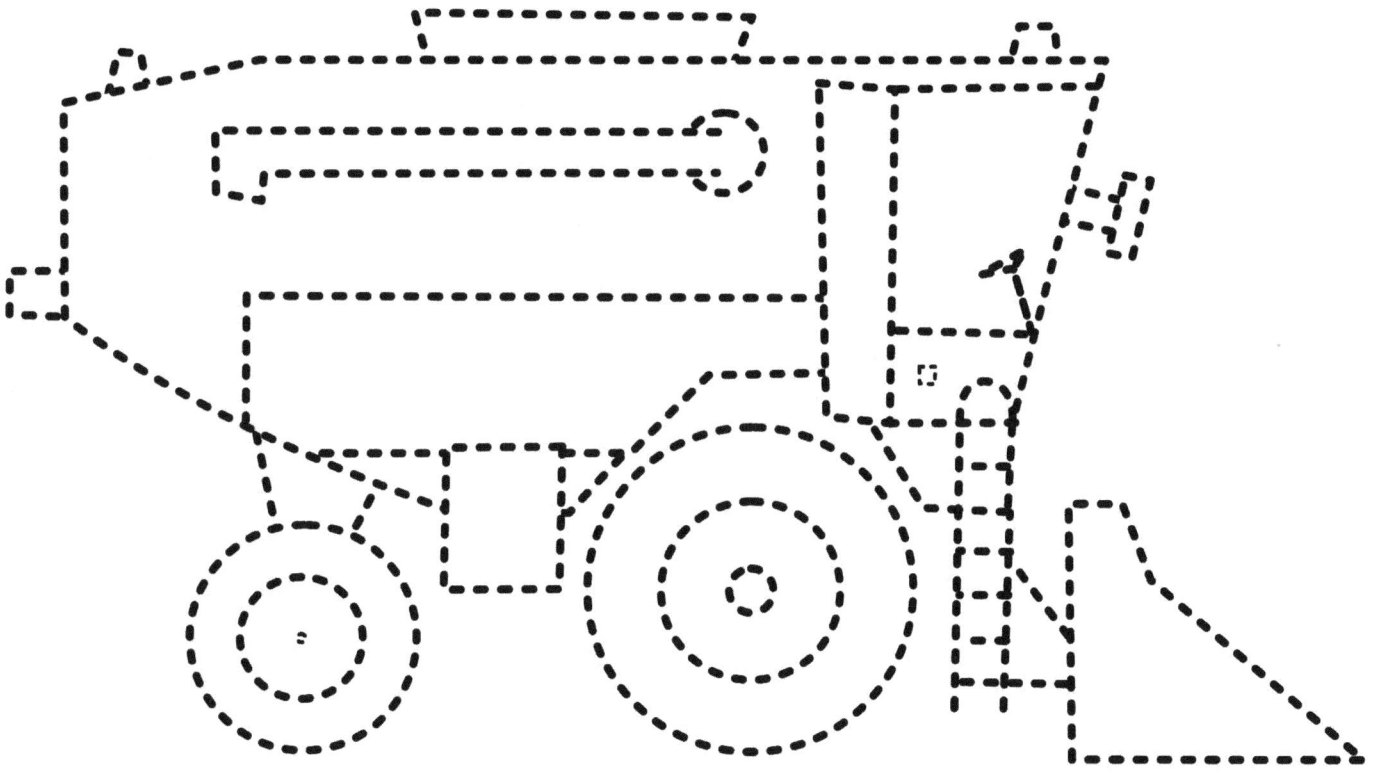

Trace.

Draw your own harvester.

Ice Resurfacing Machine

Driving Skills

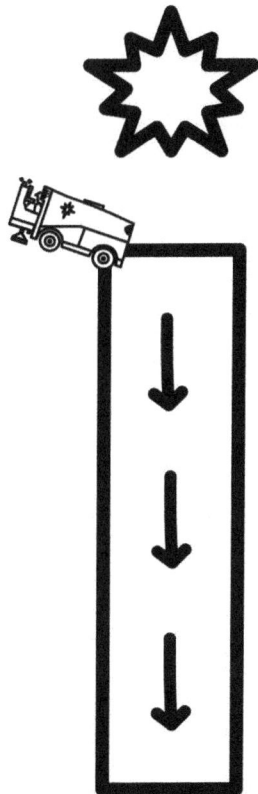

Ice Resurfacing Machine

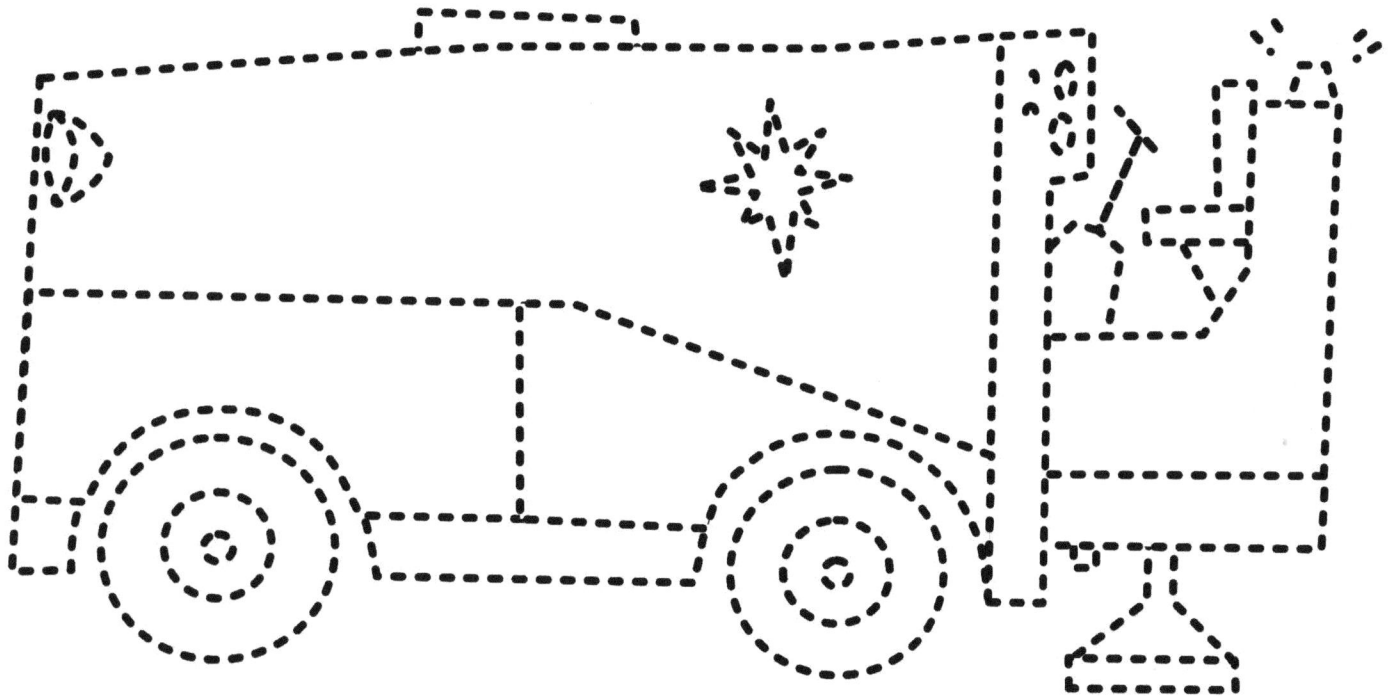

Trace.

Draw your own ice resurfacing machine.

Jack-Knife

Driving Skills

Jack-Knife

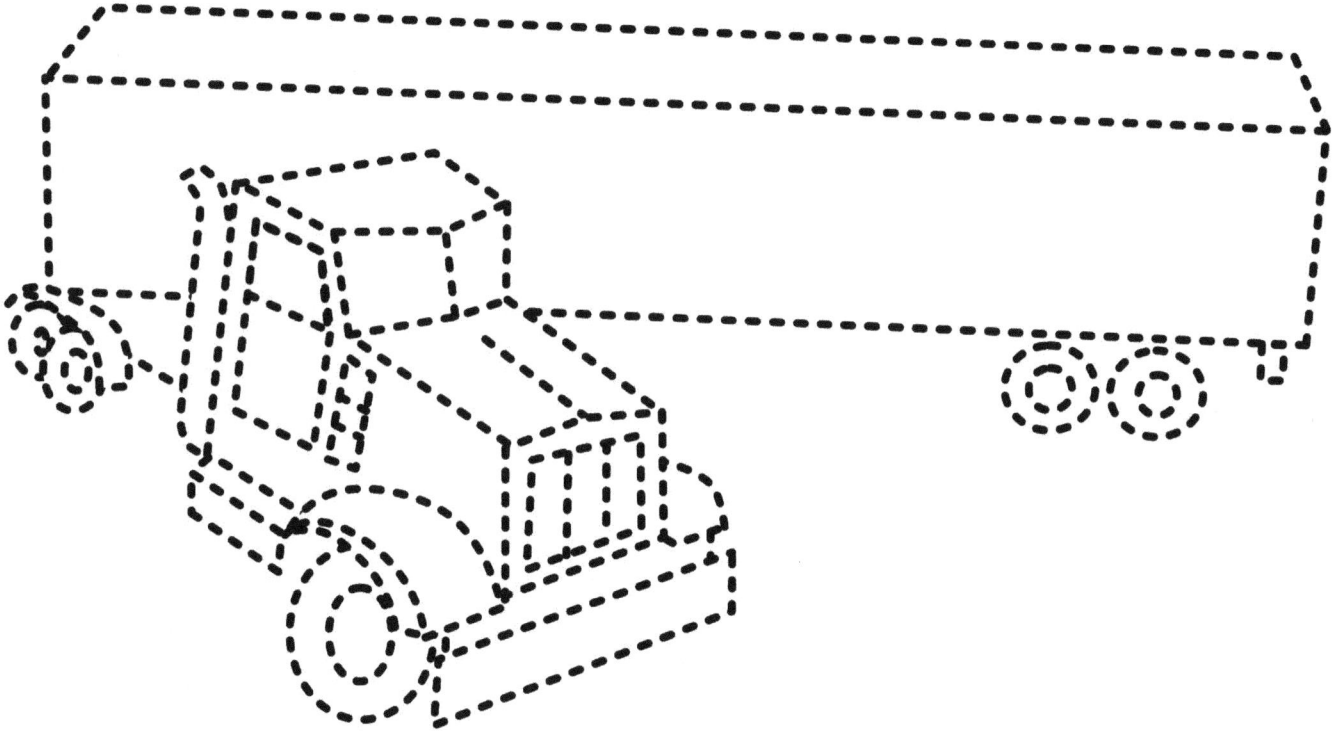

Trace.

Draw your own jack-knifed truck.

Logging Truck

Driving Skills

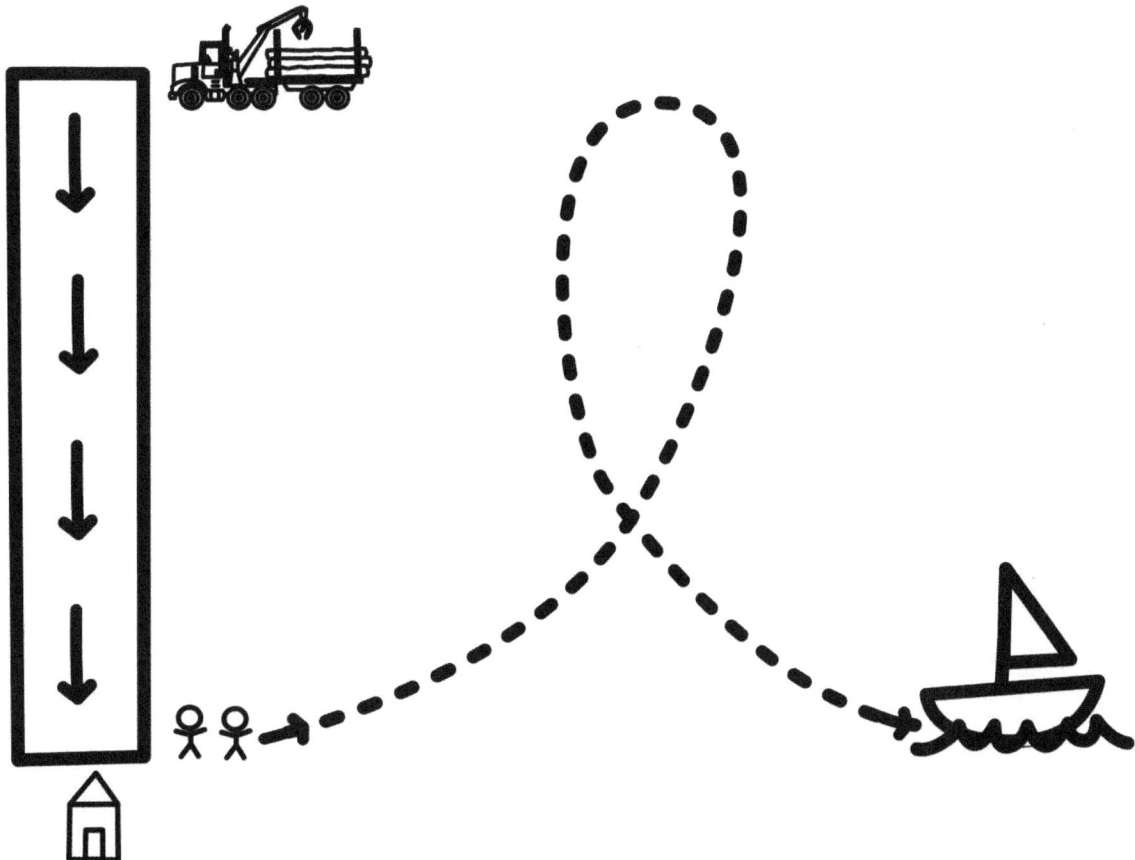

Logging Truck

Trace.

Draw your own logging truck.

Monster Truck

Driving Skills

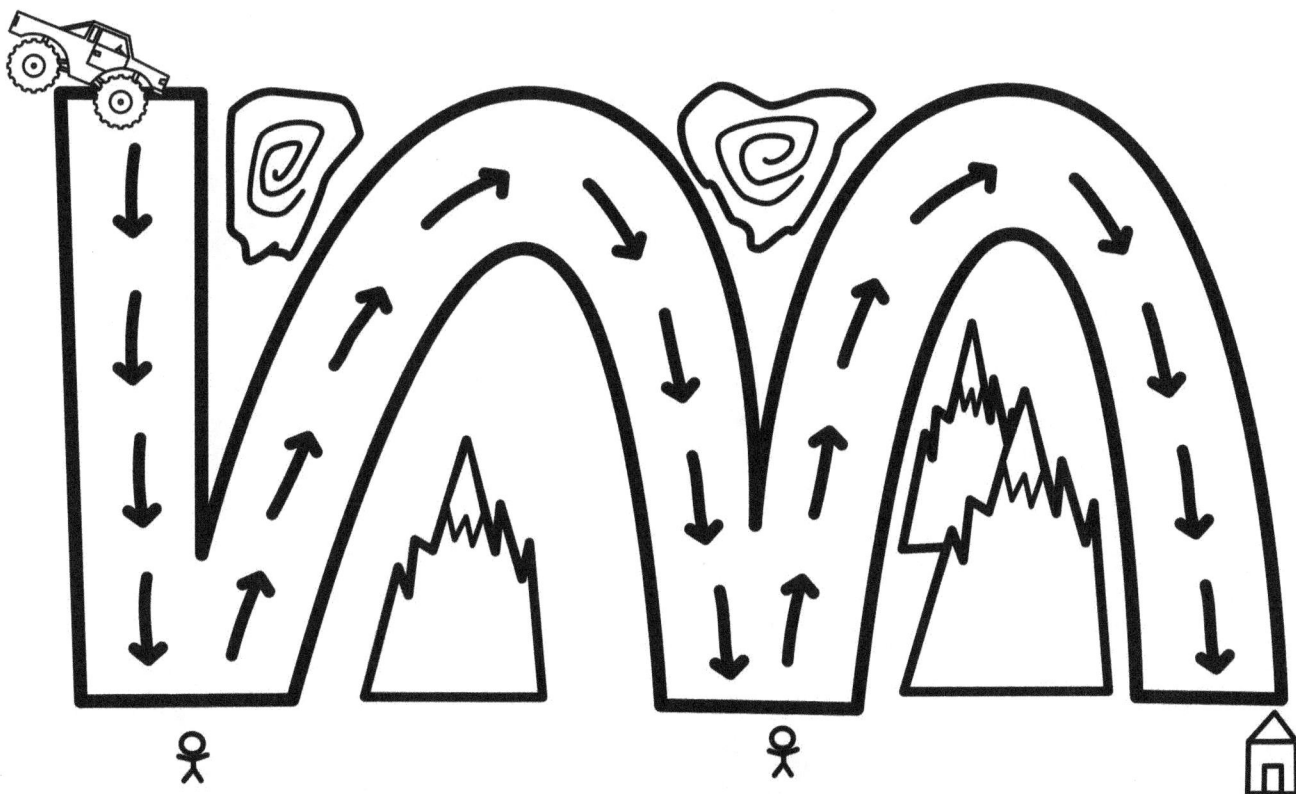

Monster Truck

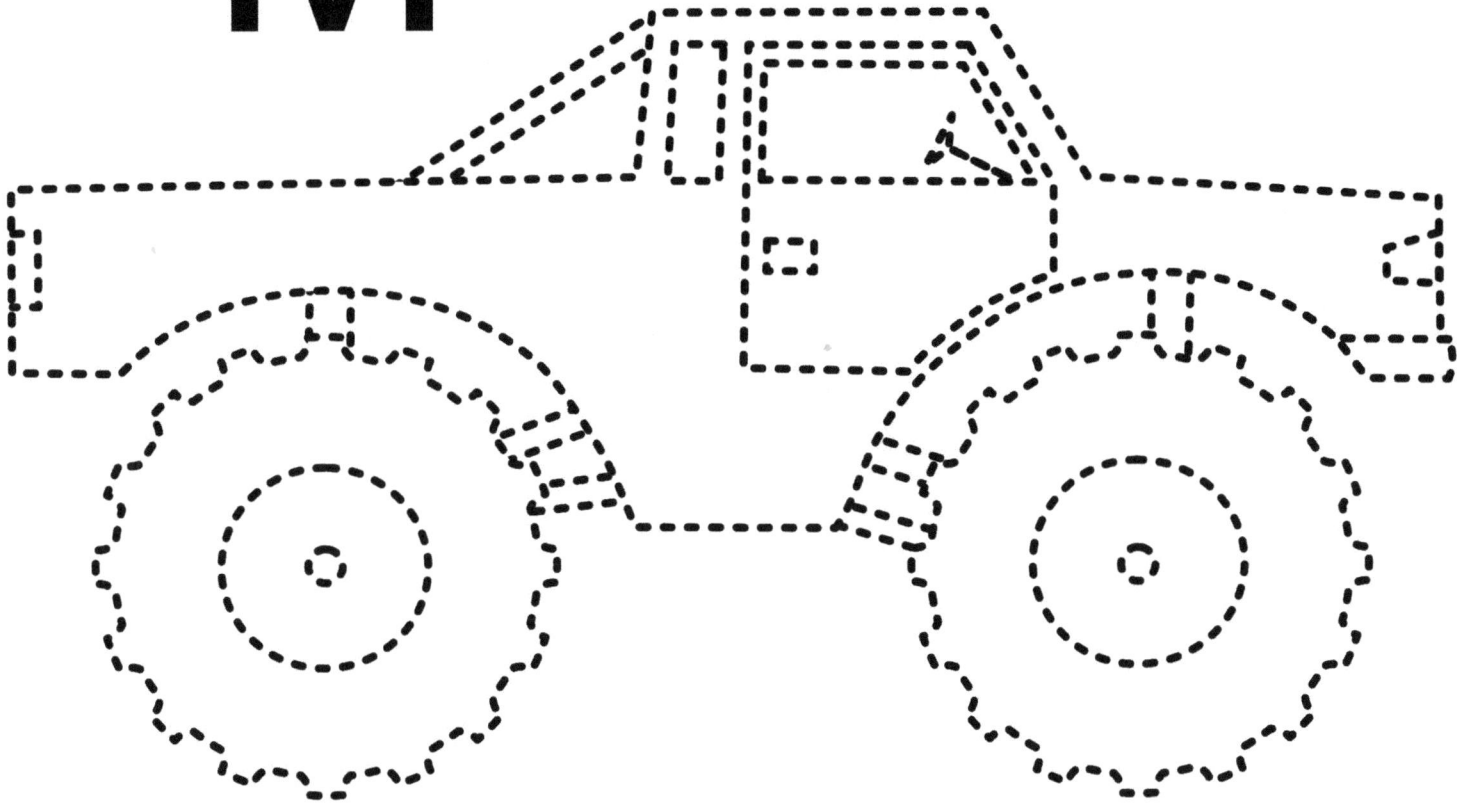

Trace.

Draw your own monster truck.

Needlenose

Driving Skills

Needlenose

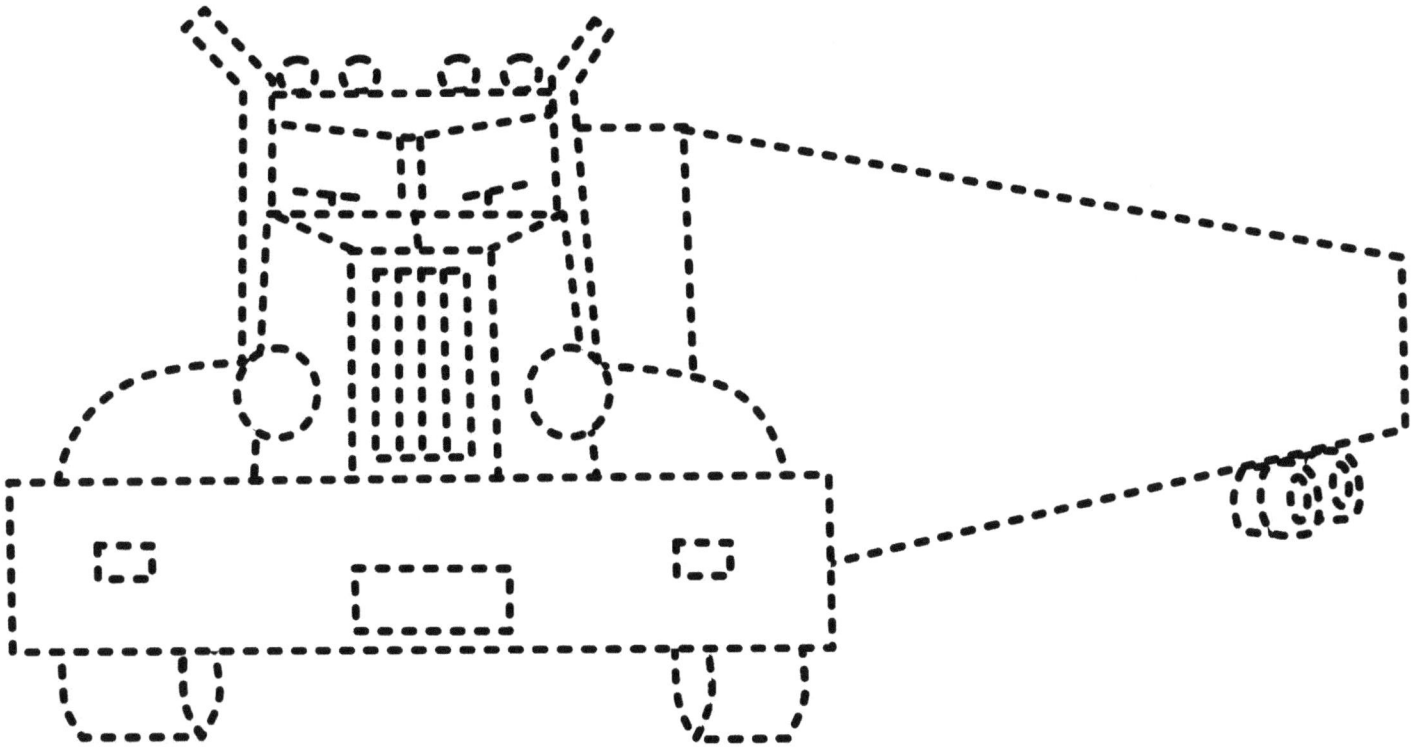

Trace.

Draw your own needlenose truck.

Off Road Vehicle

Driving Skills

Off Road Vehicle

Trace.

Draw your own off road vehicle.

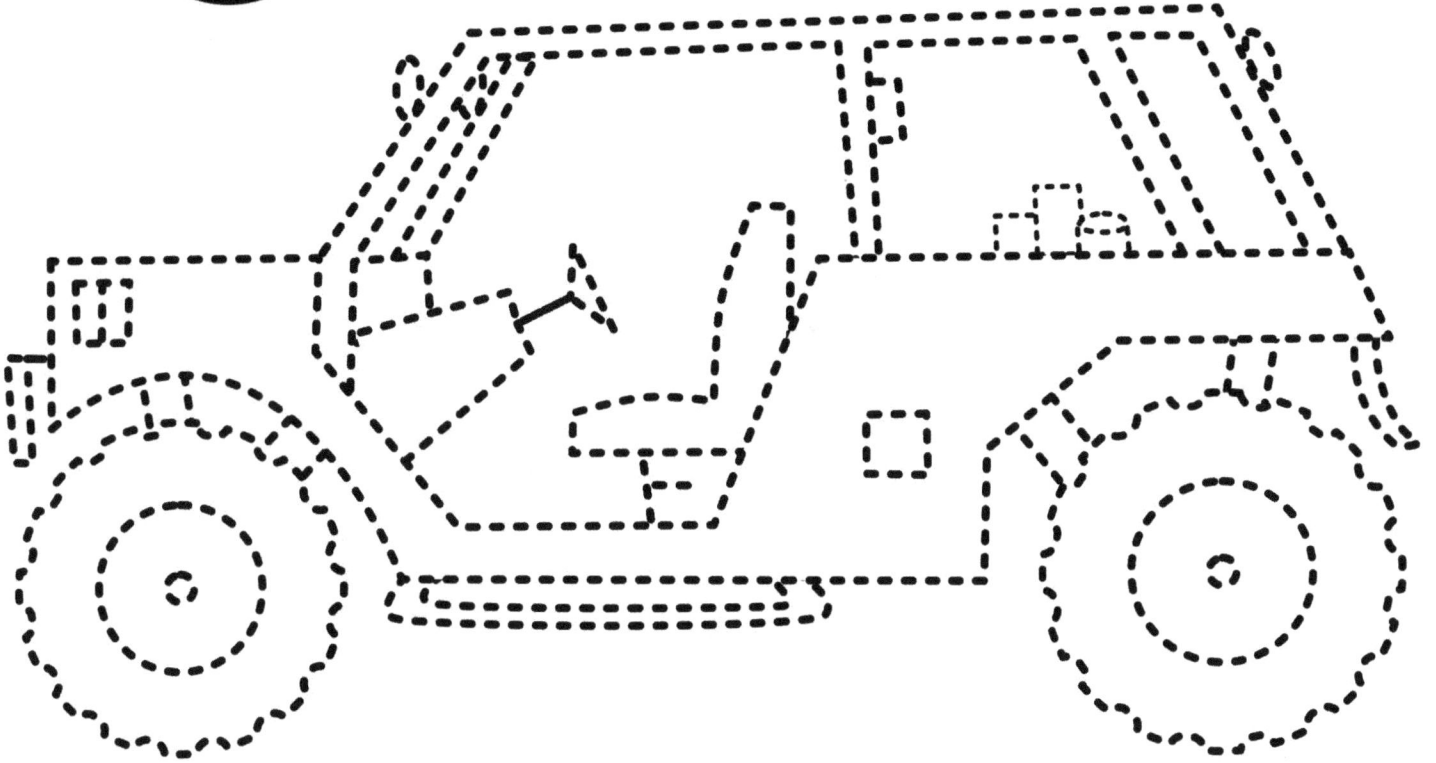

Paver

Driving Skills

Paver

Trace.

Draw your own paver.

Quad

Driving Skills

Quad

Trace.

Draw your own quad.

Road Roller

Driving Skills

Road Roller

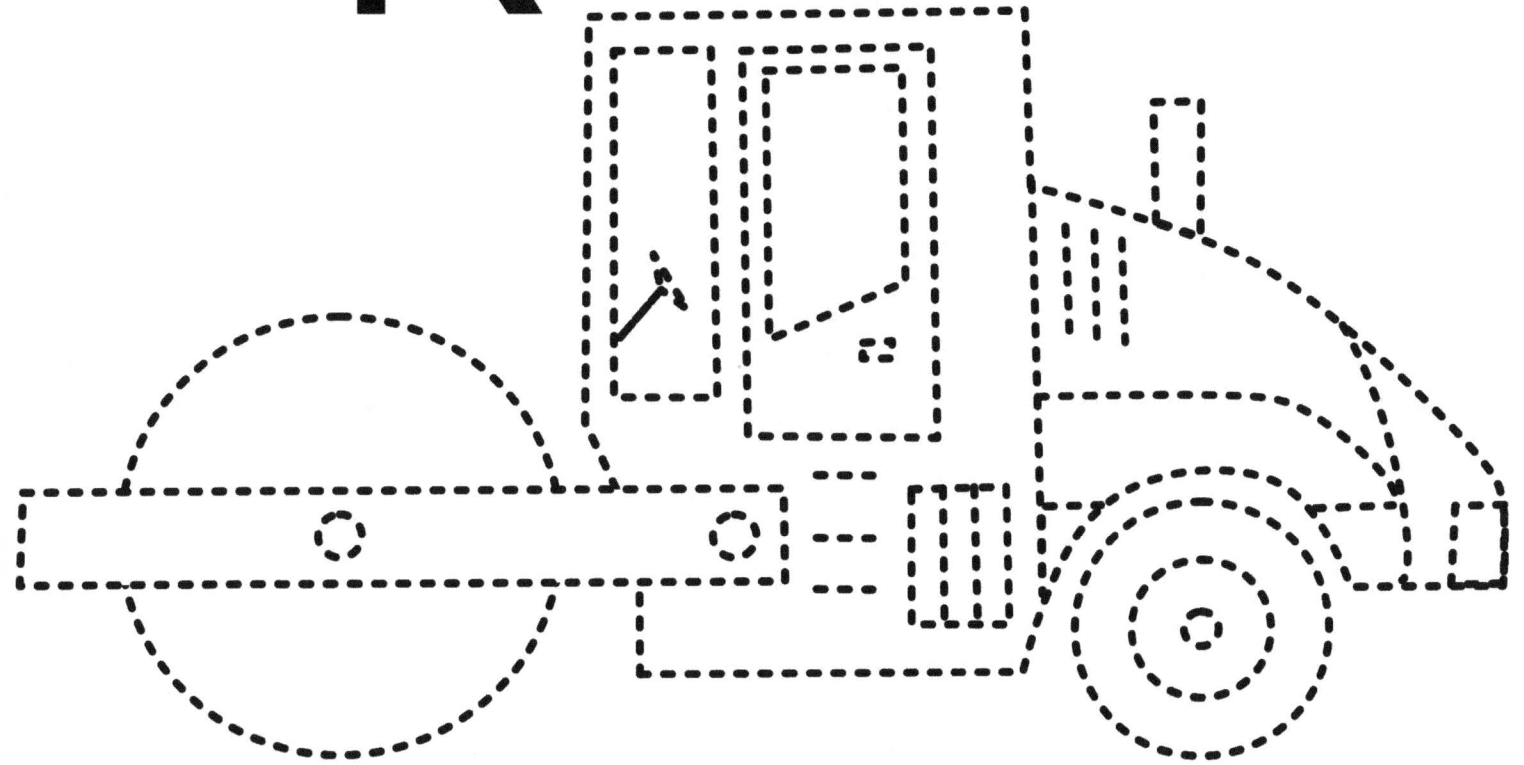

Trace.

Draw your own road roller.

Skid Steer

Driving Skills

Skid Steer

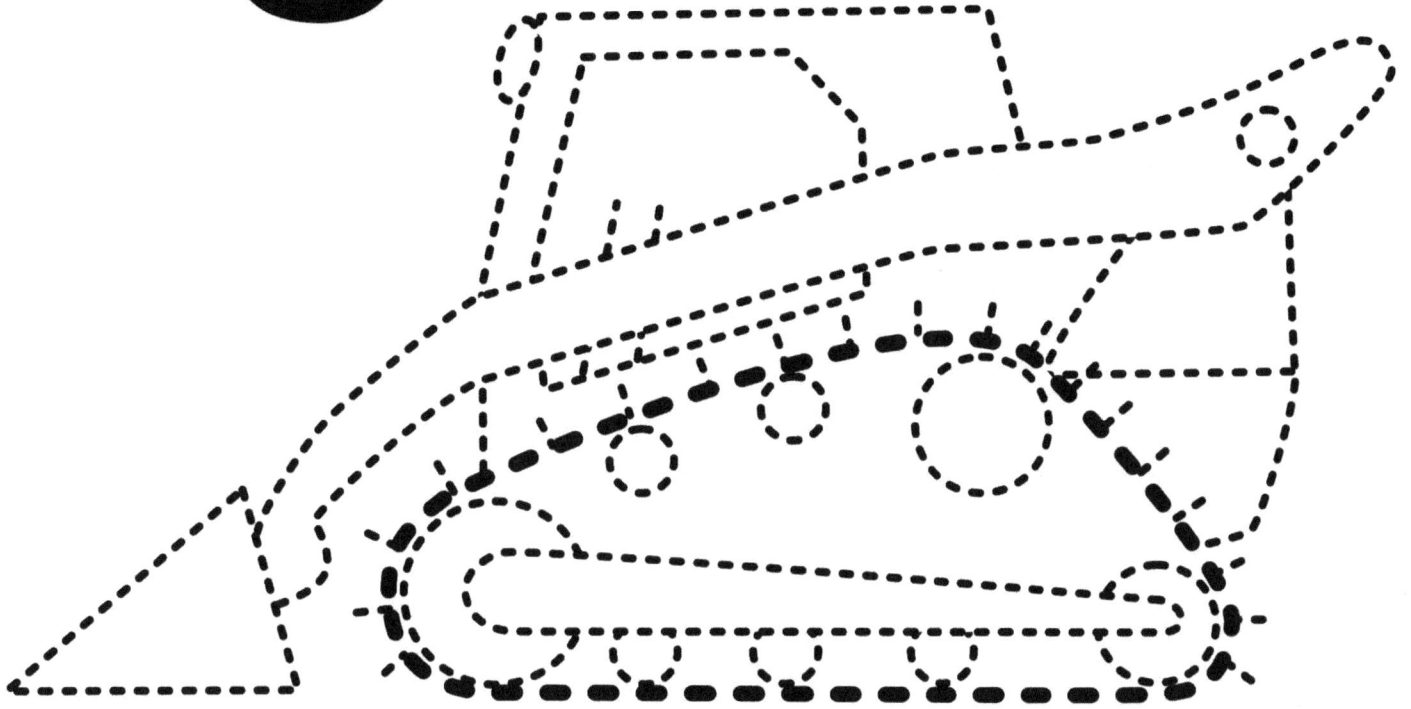

Trace.

Draw your own skid steer.

Telescopic Handler

Driving Skills

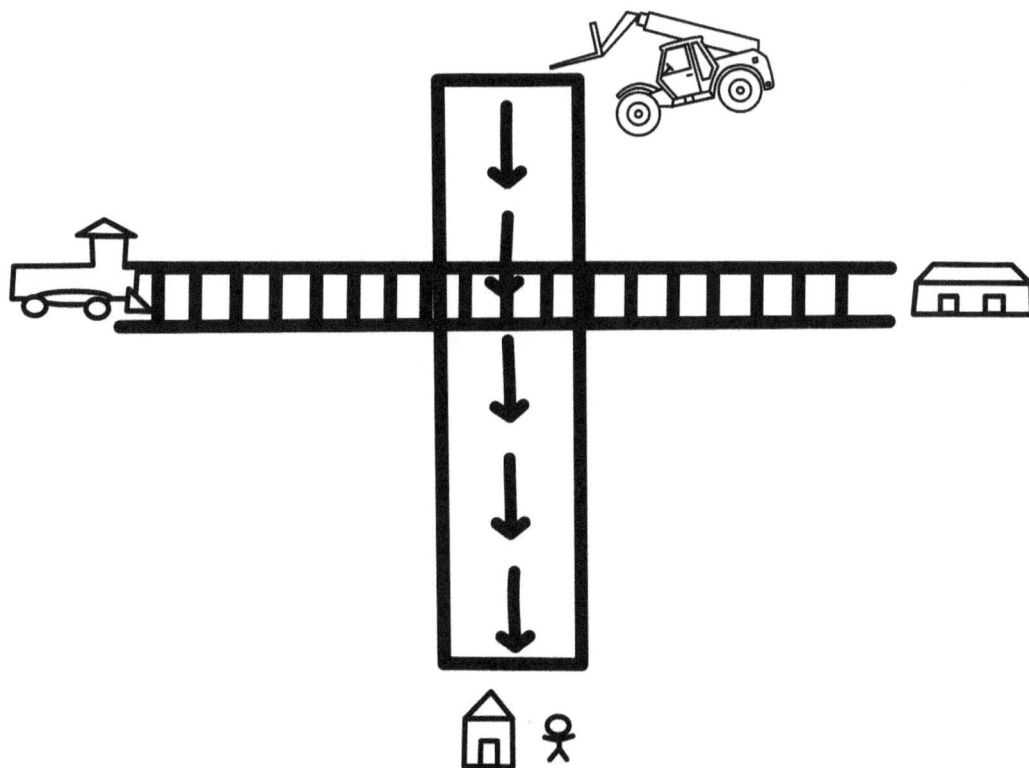

Telescopic Handler

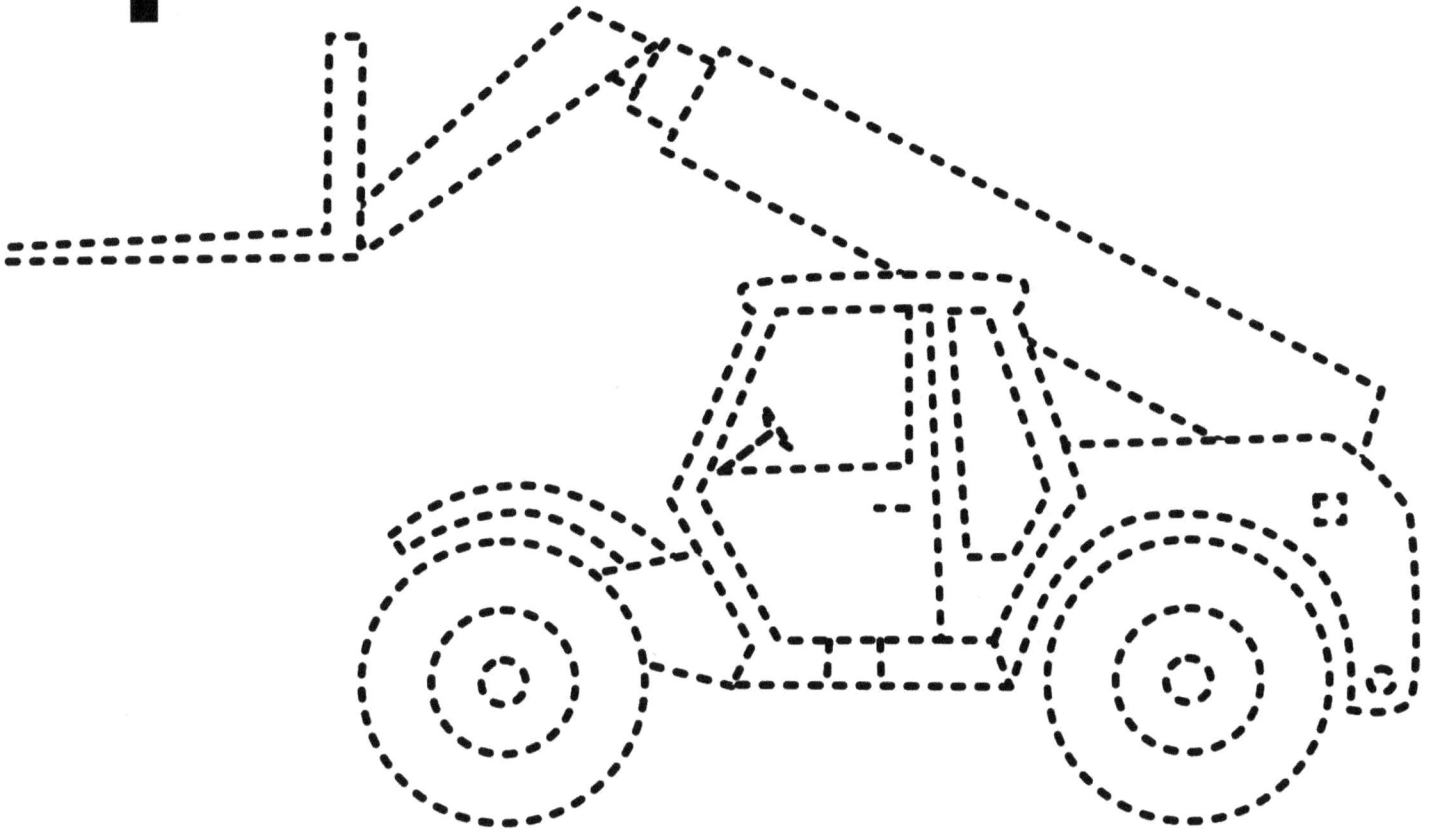

Trace.

Draw your own telescopic handler.

Utility Truck

Driving Skills

Utility Truck

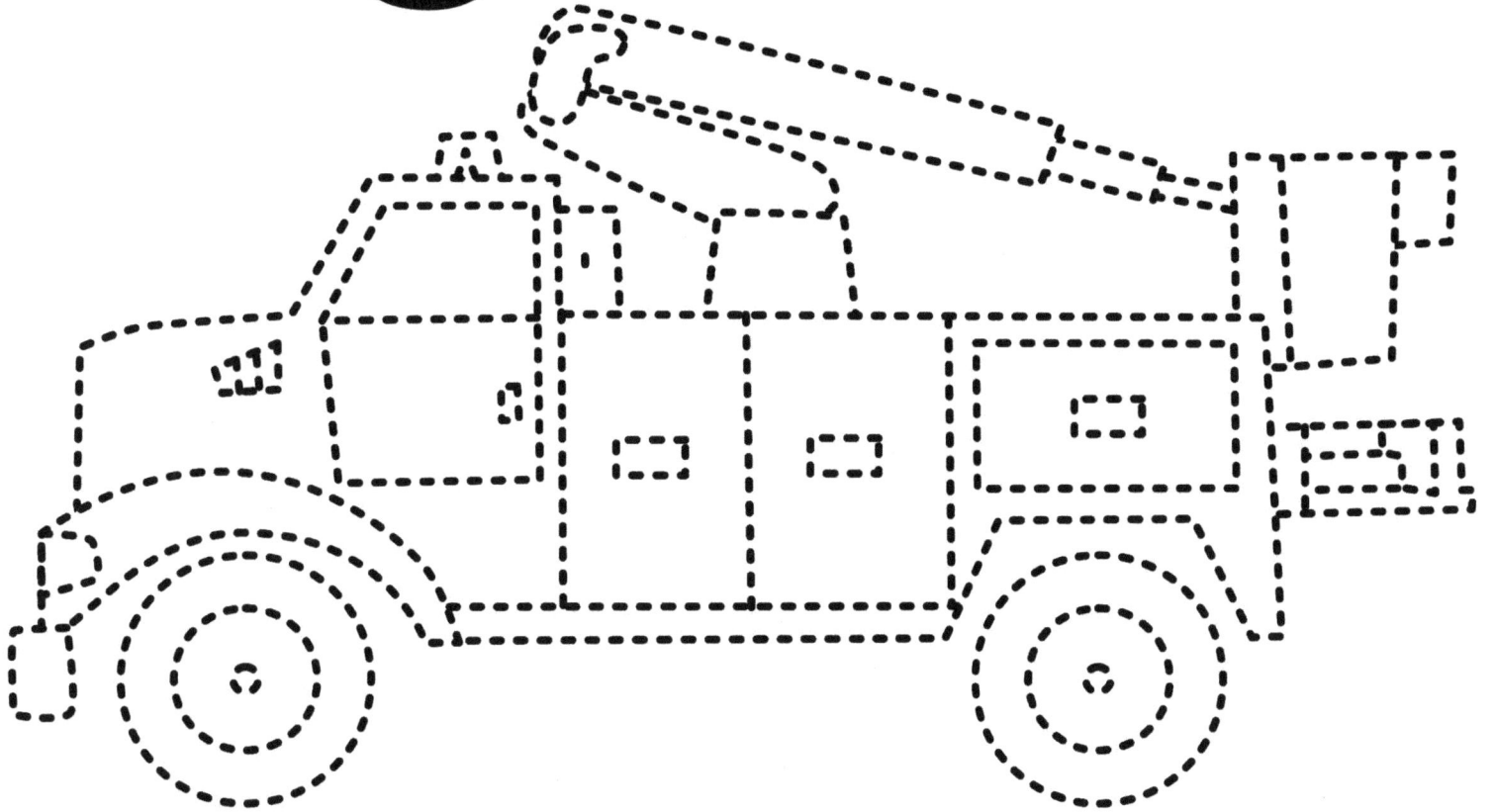

Trace.

Draw your own utility truck.

Vacuum Truck

Driving Skills

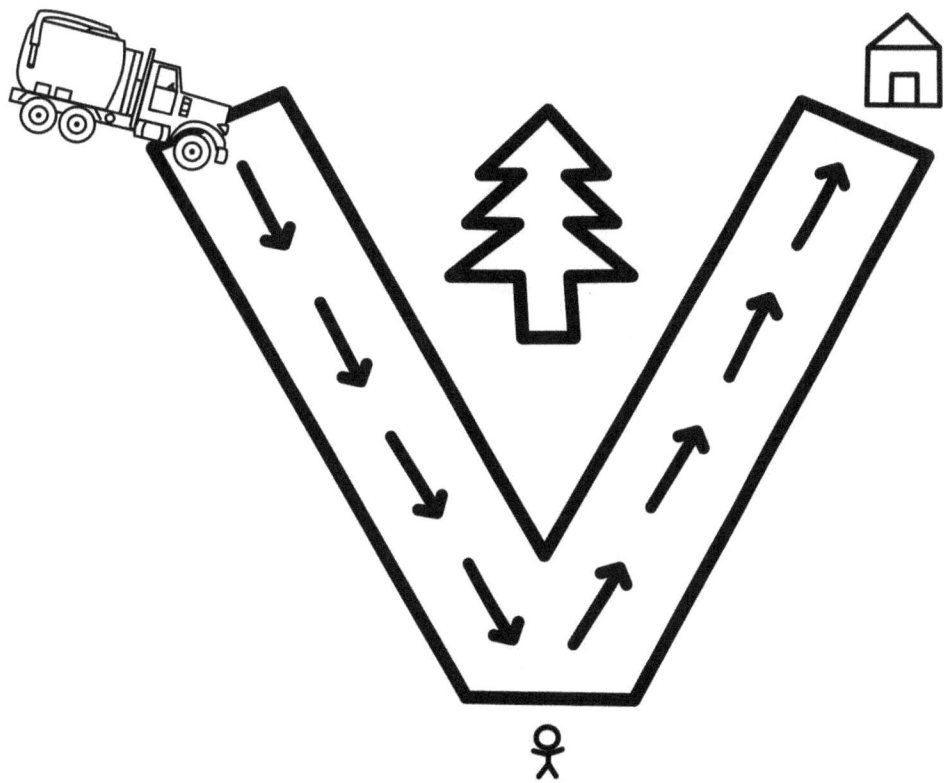

Vacuum Truck

Trace.

Draw your own vacuum truck.

Wrecker

Driving Skills

Wrecker

Trace.

Draw your own wrecker.

Bo X Truck

BOX

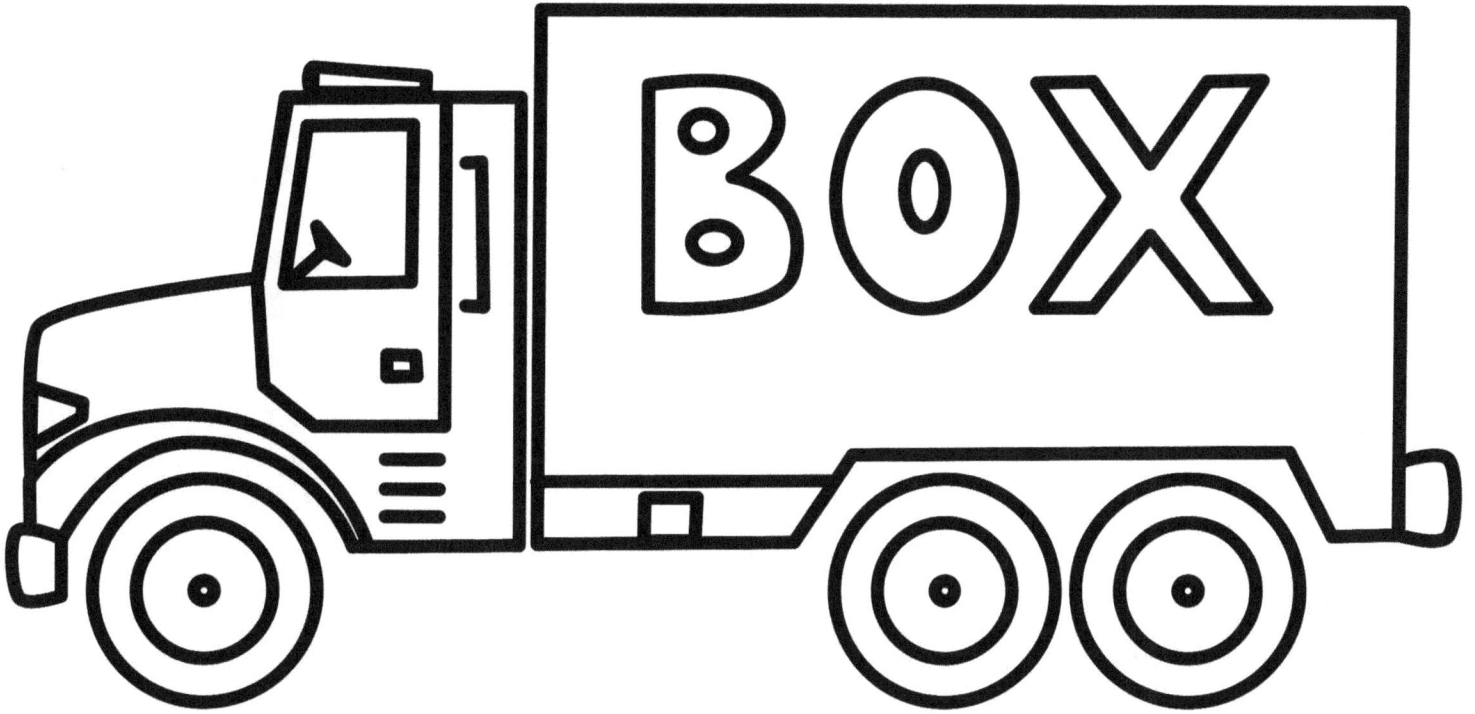

Driving Skills

Bo**X** Truck

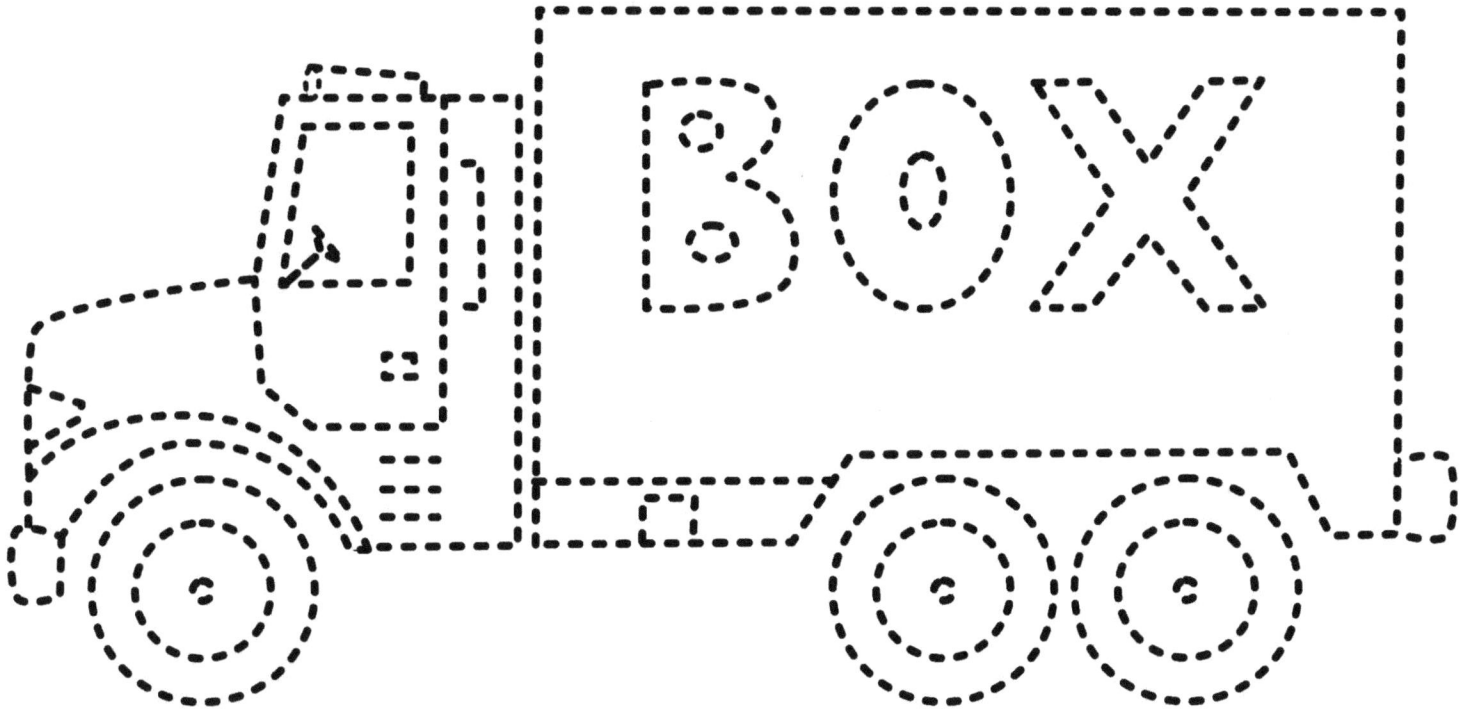

Trace.

Draw your own box truck.

Yuke

Driving Skills

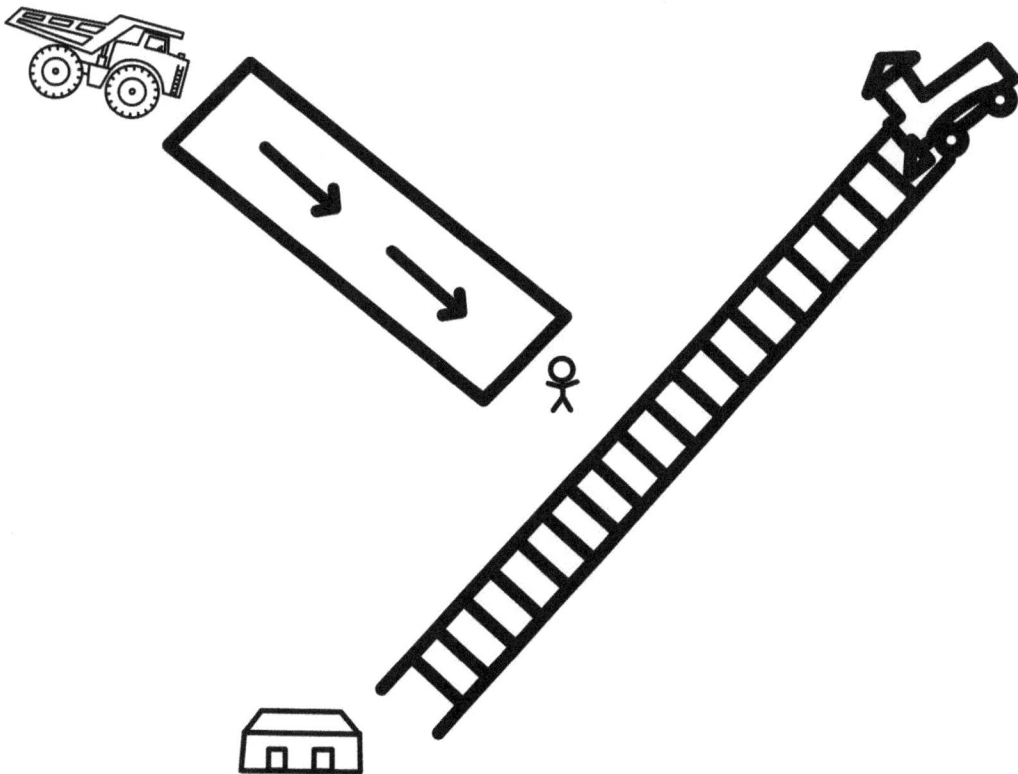

Yuke

Trace.

Draw your own yuke.

Zipper Truck

Driving Skills

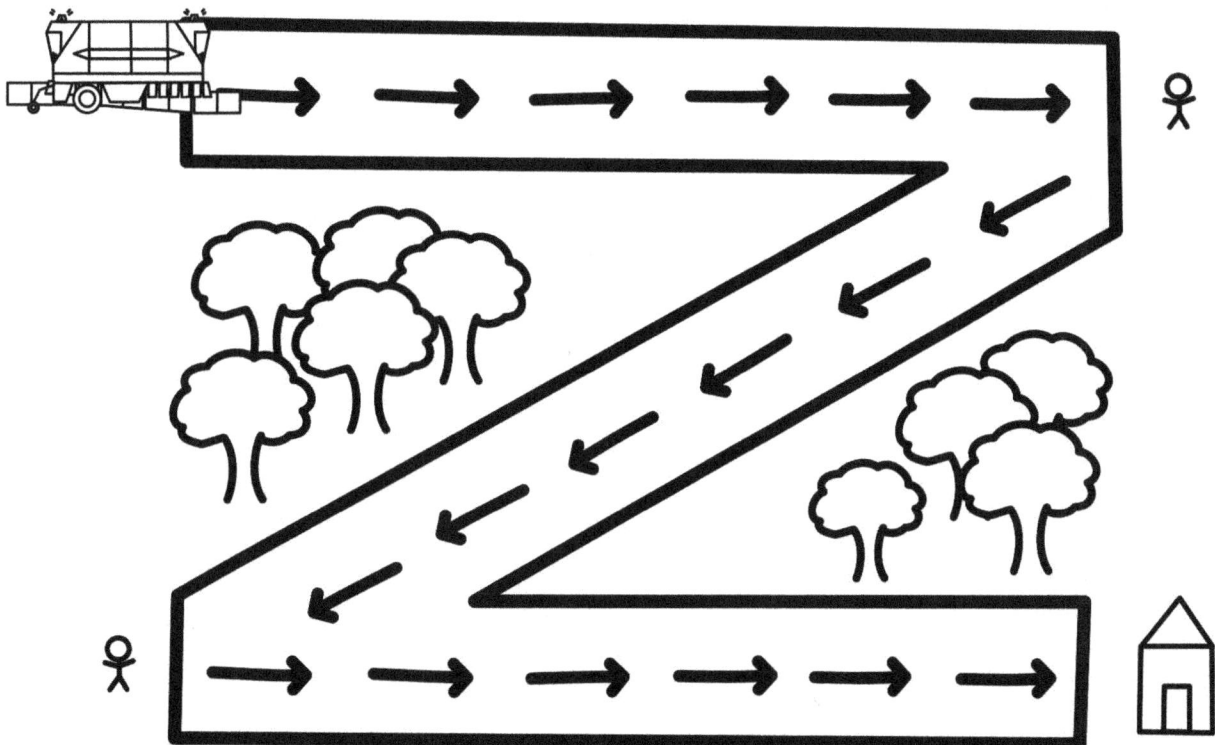

Zipper Truck

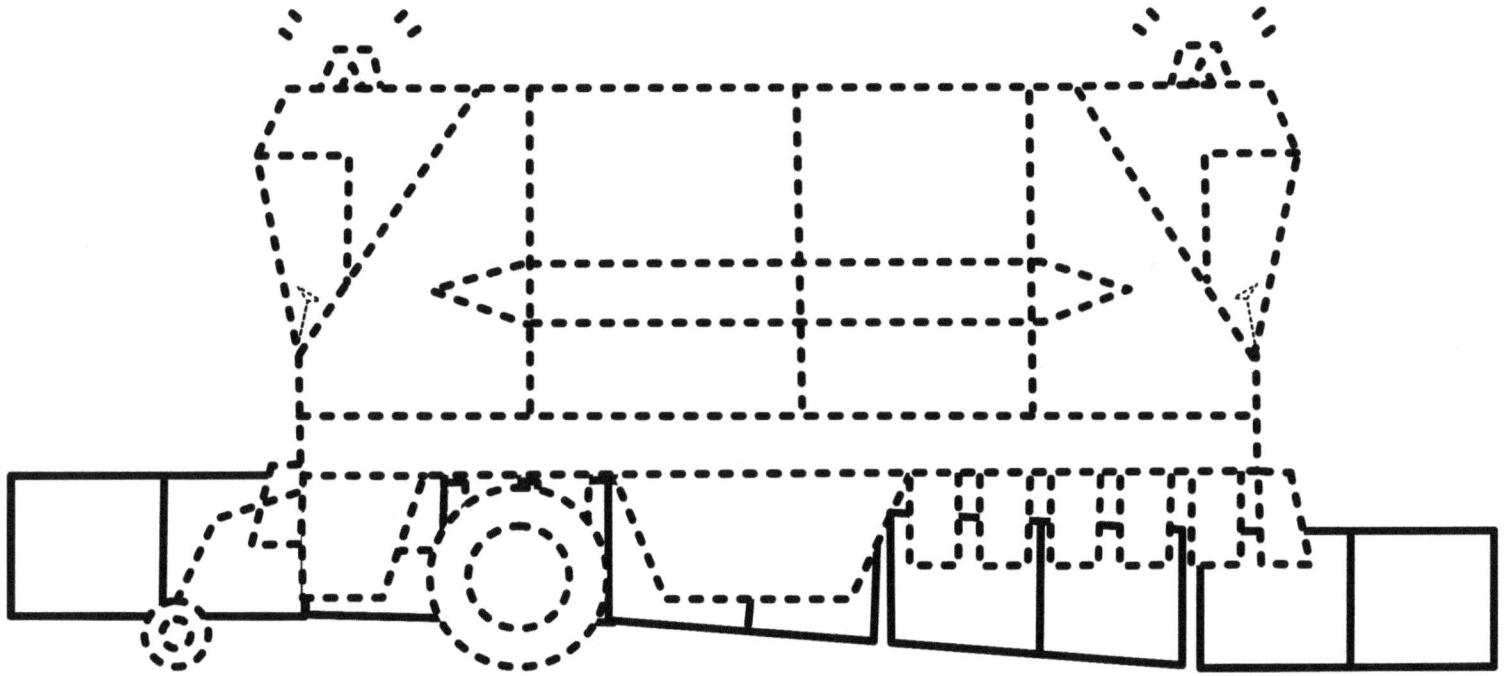

Trace.

Draw your own zipper truck.

--Master Driving Skills --

www.ingramcontent.com/pod-product-compliance
Lightning Source LLC
Chambersburg PA
CBHW081217020426
42331CB00012B/3042